T0026437

THE PERFUME OF THE CENTURY

N°5
CHANEL
PARIS

PARFUM

"A perfume is something
which is invisible and yet
an unforgettable accessory of fashion
that heralds your arrival
and prolongs your departure."

(Coco Chanel)

CONTENTS

Text by Chiara Pasqualetti Johnson

INTRODUCTION

It's been a century since the iconic perfume was launched on the market in 1921. But in the collective imagination, Chanel No. 5 is still today a perfume par excellence, one that everyone is familiar with even if they've never used it. It has resisted the whims of the fashion industry and the passing of time, as if Coco Chanel had discovered the formula for eternal femininity. It embodied the revolutionary spirit of the "Mademoiselle" as well as the atmosphere of the 1920s, an era in which a new generation of women started to stand out, women who were freer, more confident, and modern. Having finally taken charge of their own destiny, these women were ready to rebel against a life of restrictions symbolically represented by the uncomfortable corsets that Chanel abolished with her first collections, creating instead a comfortable and chic look that became emblematic of her style. However, it was its irresistible perfume more so than its fashion that transformed the Chanel name into a legend. Over time, Chanel No. 5 would become its own creature, with its own identity and history. Its simultaneously clean yet sensual bouquet was a historic turning point in the world of perfumery, and it is still today one of the most desired fragrances in the world.

N° 5

It is said that the perfume is sold at a shocking rate of one bottle every 33 seconds. However, the exact numbers, along with many other secrets regarding the perfume, are scrupulously safeguarded by Maison Chanel. Due to its fame, the true story of the incredible *monstre*, as it is reverently called by insiders, is entangled with fantasy and imagination. Decade after decade, the myth surrounding it made Chanel No. 5 much more than a simple perfume, transforming it into a cultural and social symbol that inspired artists, photographers, and directors. Much of its success derives from the infinite number of interpretations given to the plain pharmacy bottle that holds the amber liquid. As simple as a work of abstract art, its unmistakable silhouette has come to be identified with the perfume itself, so much so that when one thinks of Chanel No. 5, the first thought that comes to mind is not its scent but its iconic bottle. Few could actually identify the fragrance without seeing that transparent bottle with the interlocking Cs on the cap. The object is so recognizable that it became a trade good during World War II and a pop icon in Andy Warhol's screen prints. And eventually it became what it is today, a global obsession of the senses, a soft whisper that signifies the presence of something rich and sensual, indulgence in pleasure, the scent of one's dreams.

COCO CHANEL: THE STYLE OF AN ERA

Mademoiselle Coco Chanel rose out of extreme poverty to become the queen of haute couture. She revolutionized the concept of feminine elegance with her linear dresses and taught women the secrets of timeless elegance because "fashion changes, but style endures."

Every legend has a beginning. The story of Chanel No. 5 starts with the birth of its creator, a woman with a rousing personality and a romantic personal life. "I don't regret anything in my life except the things I didn't do," she said, and she sure did many things.

Born in 1883 in a small town in western France, she had little hope of rising out of the poor social conditions of a family of humble origins like hers. In the convent of Aubazine, where her father, a widower with five children, had left her, she came to appreciate the charm in the simplicity of the black and white tunics of the monks and also learned to sew, her ticket to her first modest job in a corsetry shop. At the time, she still went by Gabrielle, and in the evenings, after work, she would perform in *café-concerts*, where she liked to sing the song *Qui qu'a vu Coco*, giving her the nickname that would go down in history.

Coco Chanel in 1936 with her classic six strings of pearls. She was very superstitious and considered it a good luck charm to be worn both during the day and in the evening and to brighten the striking black of her clothes.

Having little talent but extraordinary vitality, she was a star in that underworld of questionable reputation, where girls were courted by young army officers, like the handsome Étienne Balsan, a tireless admirer who invited Coco to live in his château. She seized the opportunity to escape poverty with a tenacity that demonstrated her strength of character, imagining a different future from the one she seemed destined for. At Balsan's château, she met a wealthy member of the upper class from Newcastle, England, Arthur "Boy" Capel. Their grand love story would have a tragic fate but was also the springboard for the launch of the Chanel brand. Thanks to Boy's help, Coco started her first milliner's shop on rue Cambon in Paris, an address that would end up in the history books as the home of Maison Chanel. There, Mademoiselle began her compelling ascent. She made simple straw hats, a complete contrast to the opulence that was prevalent during the Belle Époque. They already had that unique, elegant, and linear style that would become characteristic of every fiber of her clothing. In 1913, she opened a second boutique in Deauville, a sophisticated seaside location, then a third in the elite town of Biarritz.

"A man can wear what he wants; he'll always be a woman's accessory."

In the '20s, her style triumphed, defeating the nineteenth-century idea of femininity. "A man can wear what he wants; he'll always be a woman's accessory," Coco would say as she wreaked havoc on women's wardrobes, dropping the hemline of skirts to below the knees, lowering the waistline, and inventing the little black dress, a quintessential part of chic Parisian style. This simple dress threw out the constraints of the corset. *Vogue* compared it to a Ford T, something the world from then on could not do without. From rummaging through the closets of her lovers, she introduced the use of pants and tweed, transforming the most masculine of fabrics into soft female jackets. Having achieved wealth and fame, her ambiguous and slightly androgynous allure grew, her boyish haircut being as popular as her clothes. It was a hit in the most famous salons, where gossipers whispered about the relationships she was believed to have had with men and women, artists and aristocrats. She was a friend of Stravinsky's and Picasso's and even won over Cocteau, who said, "Your work is a kind of miracle. You have worked in fashion according to rules that would seem to have value only for painters, musicians, and poets."

Coco was at the height of her career when word began to spread that she was apparently sympathetic to the Fascist movement. With the start of World War II, she decided to disappear, but it was not goodbye. In 1955, at seventy, Coco returned to her work, challenging the new look of Christian Dior's full skirts with her dainty pantsuits, which immediately became part of the closets of stars. Her name became synonymous with her interlocking CC monogram, the first logo in fashion history; the 2.55 quilted leather handbags; and the two-tone pumps, half beige to make the leg look longer and half black to make the foot look smaller and hide dirt. The camellia also become synonymous with the woman. The geometrically perfect Chinese flower adorned the Coromandel room dividers that surrounded her in her suite at the Ritz Hotel, where she lived almost all her life. After a fairytale life, she died on January 10, 1971, a Sunday, her least favorite day of the week because it required one to be uselessly idle, something that was inconceivable for a woman whose work was her reason for living.

THE SCENT OF A WOMAN, THE BIRTH OF A LEGEND

A love story, a Russian prince, and the perfumer of the tsars. The idea to create a perfume for Maison Chanel was born in the flower fields of Provence. It was 1921, and the world would never be the same again.

In the 1920s, immediately after the end of World War I, the world was ready for a new revolution. Albert Einstein had won the Nobel Prize in Physics, the miracle of vaccines had eradicated deadly illnesses that were destroying the population, and Lindbergh flew across the Atlantic from New York to Paris in less than 34 hours. There were wireless radios and spoken films, rumbling cars, and the sparkling windows of department stores. The economy was racing to achieve new standards of luxury and well-being that even reached part of the middle class for the first time. Coco Chanel chose this moment, in which the world chased modernity, to launch her Maison's perfume. The way it happened is one of the most fascinating chapters in perfumery history, and the result would be revolutionary, obscuring everything that had occurred previously.

Her fated meeting with the Russian Grand Duke Dmitri Pavlovich took place in the cosmopolitan atmosphere of Venice in the 1920s, a capital of eccentric glamour, masquerade parties, and fallen nobility, where fascinating strangers rubbed shoulders. A cousin of Tsar Nicholas II's, Dmitri was one of the exiled instigators of the murder of Rasputin, which meant he barely escaped before the Russian Revolution. Coco was won over by his pale face, which gave him the air of a romantic hero. She was crazy for this man 11 years her junior. They started a relationship that would last less than a year during 1921, a fundamental year for Chanel's future. Their idyllic life had just begun when they spent a romantic vacation in Grasse. It was there that Dmitri introduced her to Ernest Beaux, the perfumer of the tsars who sought refuge there, the global capital of perfumery, after having escaped from Saint Petersburg. It was there, among the flower fields of Provence, that the idea to create a perfume for Chanel was born.

Coco and the Grand Duke Dmitri Pavlovich, cousin of Tsar Nicholas II, in 1920 during their love affair.

Coco knew she wanted something extraordinary. And Beaux was unfazed. He was familiar with the requests of demanding clients like Mademoiselle after serving the tsarina of Russia for years, for whom he had created a legendary fragrance called the Bouquet de Catherine in honor of Catherine the Great. Between summer and fall of 1920, he developed several blends before giving Coco two sets of samples that she could choose from. The vials were numbered 1 to 5 and 20 to 24 and contained different combinations of around 80 ingredients. They were only apparently similar as each emitted a variation of the symphony of scents. Coco was convinced: number 5. All she had to do was choose a name for the new perfume. Since her fashion house was already famous, she decided to simply call it Chanel, fully taking advantage of the fame of its name. Forward-thinking as always, she also knew she needed to distinguish this first perfume more specifically in case she were to ever create another. Since she had chosen sample number 5, why not call it Chanel No. 5?

The number five, after all, had always been her lucky number. Coco believed in the magic and beauty of numbers, and five represented the purest, most quintessential embodiment of the essence of a body. It probably also reminded her of the use of numbered patterns on the stone floors of the old Aubazine Abbey, the orphanage she grew up in. As an adult, she began reproducing it everywhere, even in her apartment in rue Cambon, where the number 5 popped up in the most unthinkable of places, like between the rock crystal teardrops in the living room chandelier. The number was so special that she always chose it for the dates of her fashion shows, persistently scheduled for February 5 and August 5. The quote that would go down in history, although possibly incorrectly passed down, was something Coco said to Ernest Beaux: "I present my dress collections on the fifth of May, the fifth month of the year, and so we will let this sample number five keep the name it already has; it will bring good luck."

When it was ready, she cleverly decided not to immediately display the bottle in shop windows. Instead, she invited a close circle of influential friends to a restaurant in Cannes and sprayed the perfume in the air. "All the women who passed by our table stopped to smell the unusual fragrance while we acted as if it was nothing," she said, remembering the moment.

Soon after, she gave it to her chicest friends, counting on word of mouth to spread about it, a powerful method of promotion. When the women came to her store to ask for another bottle of the magnificent fragrance, Coco feigned shock, saying she hadn't thought about selling it and

Ernest Beaux, the perfumer of the tsars who created the revolutionary bouquet of Chanel No. 5.

that it was just a souvenir, feeding the infallible correlation between desire and availability. When it was finally put on display, it immediately flew off the shelves in the hands of Europe's elegant elite. At the beginning, it appeared only discreetly on the shelves of Chanel boutiques, where it was sprayed abundantly, enveloping the clothes in a fragrant cloud. It would sell out in a matter of days. The first samples were produced by the company Rallet, a small Provençal company where Ernest Beaux was working. But Coco wasn't happy because many bottles were defective and Rallet couldn't keep up with the timing of the increasing number of orders.

She thus decided to turn to Pierre and Paul Wertheimer, the brilliant owners of Bourjois, a cosmetic industry giant. In 1924, she started the Chanel Société des Parfums with them. Coco and the Wertheimers were partners, and Ernest was the technical director. Although she was smart with numbers, Coco was unfamiliar with any financial aspect and bored by bills and statements.

She detested having to manage the business side of things. The agreement thus established that Coco would not deal with administrative and commercial affairs for the perfume but that she would receive 10% of profits every year from Chanel Parfums, income that she benefited from the rest of her life, meaning she'd want for nothing. The agreement was renegotiated after a bitter legal battle in 1946, which no longer gave her a right to a percentage of the profits but rather 2% of global sales, a significant increase in her earnings. Poverty was now nothing more than a mere memory. Coco Chanel had become one of the richest women in the world. What started as a drop of perfume transformed into a company that includes cosmetics and clothing, enormously increasing its turnover. However, Coco's objective was never to become wealthy; for her, Chanel No. 5 was the incarnation of a certain style, an essence that used the senses to reflect her aesthetic. It was extremely simple yet splendidly over the top and audacious, just like her.

SEXY AND CHIC: THE FABULOUS DESTINY OF NO. 5

What is the essence of Chanel style? A revolutionary bouquet and a transparent bottle that became an iconic work of art. Loved by artists and Hollywood superstars who made it legendary, its resounding commercial success was transformed into a social and cultural symbol.

"A women's perfume that smells like a woman." That's what Coco Chanel had
in mind when she was creating her first perfume. "I'm not looking for the smell
of roses or lily of the valley," she said as she worked with Ernest Beaux
to develop the fragrance. "I want an elaborate perfume."

The fragrance is unlike any already well-known perfume, any identifiable bouquet. It recalls the smell of clean, soapy hands, perhaps the same scent Gabrielle Chanel remembered smelling as a young girl on her mother's skin after doing laundry. However, the perfume also has a sensual and provocative aspect that makes it unique. What Coco wanted was the essence of femininity. She was definitely opposed to the smell of flowers and didn't want a boudoir scent because, at that time, a woman's reputation was unmistakably established by the trail of her perfume. Certain aromas, like jasmine and musk, patchouli and tuberose, gave women a sensuality that only an actress or courtesan would have dared to wear with confidence. Respectable women smelled like the delicate fragrances of rose and violet, which evoked the innocence of a unopened flower blossom. In her youth, when Coco frequented the *café-concert* underworld, she learned how important fragrance was in presenting (or not) one's sensuality. Although her past life was considered improper and would be a shadow she tried to distance herself from her whole life, it also

"There is nothing more mysterious, more human than the sense of smell. Thanks to smells, we know that our body corresponds to that of another."

contained pleasant memories of parties, joking, and laughing, as well as the idyllic relationship with her first great love, Boy Capel. That's why she sought to create a perfume that would definitively blur the lines of what was suitable for a respectable woman and something that was meant for a seductress. As usual, she chose to shock and awe with something that had never been done before. Chanel No. 5 is made of the perfect blend of contrasts, showing the world that a woman can be seductive and pure at the same time.

The discovery of a new ingredient was crucial to achieving this. Aldehydes are chemical compounds that give fragrances an abstract, airy, and modern allure. It was exactly what she needed to update the existing category of floral perfumes. The recipe that Ernest developed combined the main essences of rose and jasmine with 80 other ingredients, including musk, ylang-ylang, and sandalwood. The aldehydes add a note of freshness and create a pleasant sensation that bursts into a thousand champagne bubbles or a spark of electricity when smelled. It gives off the scent of clean sheets and warm bodies, evoking both purity and sensuality. When Ernest warned Coco that a perfume with so many essences would accrue exorbitant costs, she told him that was exactly what she wanted. She wished to create the most excessive perfume in the world.

Its presentation was also revolutionary and went fully against the current of fashion at that time, when the creative and overly decorated bottles of Lalique and Baccarat were the norm. The novel bouquet of natural and synthetic notes that Coco created was extraordinarily complex but was presented in contrast to a bottle that looked like something in a pharmacy. Its simple, transparent, and square-shaped form and minimal black and white label recall a modernist sculpture. Coco was obsessed with simplicity and precision. This decision revealed how much she had learned from frequently spending time with Picasso and his artist friends, so much so that the perfume looked like a piece of modern, almost abstract art.

That flair for simplicity can also be found in the label, a white rectangle with the words "No. 5 Chanel Paris" in harsh, black, sans serif lettering, like that used by the avant-garde artists. The unmistakable logo with the interlocking Cs is stamped at the base of the stopper. The white cardboard box it came

The revolutionary simplicity of the first Chanel No. 5 bottle from 1921. It was a simple pharmacy bottle with a tiny black and white label.

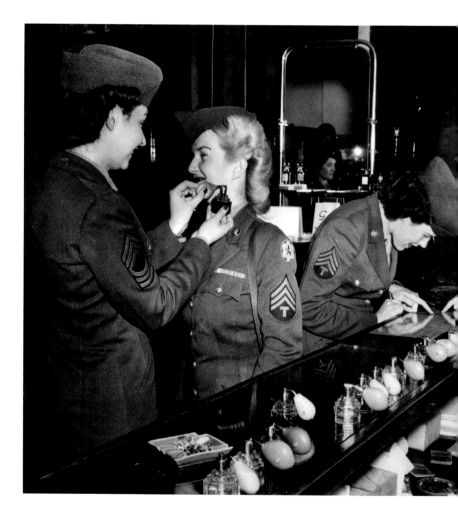

Women soldiers choose perfumes in the Chanel store on rue Cambon in 1945.

in was also shocking for that time. It was so radically simple that it was associated with the Dadaist aesthetic. It recalled the graphic design of "papillons Dada," the posters with short texts printed on cream-colored paper by artists like Tristan Tzara and Francis Picabia, who even used the number five in a piece entitled *Ticket* from 1922. After the commotion it stirred up in Paris in the mid-1920s, Chanel No. 5 began to be sold outside of France. Women raced to be the first to grab the new fragrance, which soon would become an object of desire in the rest of Europe as well. But the true success came when Chanel No. 5 landed in the United States, where women read fashion magazines like *Vogue* and would change the hemlines of their skirts according to the trends in Paris.

However, what caused the French perfume mania on the other side of the ocean was not magazines but rather American soldiers. Having arrived by the thousands in Paris in 1944 during Liberation, they would line up outside the Chanel store to ensure they got the perfect souvenir to take back to their girlfriends waiting for them at home. The entire bottom floor of the shop in rue Cambon was used to display the sparkling bottles that reflected infinitely in the surrounding mirrors. The soldiers didn't speak a word of French, but all they needed was to raise five fingers to receive their own symbol of victory and elegance. The perfume was Paris. And Paris was sexy and chic. It was also sold on the black market around Europe at the same price as gold, whiskey, and cigarettes. Shortly after, Chanel No. 5 began to be distributed tax-free at Post Exchanges, military outlets for the U.S. Army. The bottle that represented quintessential French luxury had now unexpectedly become available to the middle class at a discounted price, and it ended up spreading its unmistakable scent to every corner of the globe. Its true success, however, was still to come.

A model poses while being framed by the perfume in a photo montage by Weegee in the 1950s.

A few years later, a completely unexpected incident would catapult the perfume to an unprecedented level of fame: the extraordinary, unexpected, and free publicity from Marilyn Monroe in 1952. When an indiscreet journalist from *Life* magazine asked her what she wore to bed, she responded, "Nothing but a few drops of Chanel No. 5."

Marilyn Monroe with a Chanel No. 5 bottle in a famous photo by Ed Feingersh in 1955.

*"What do I wear to bed? Nothing
but a few drops of Chanel No. 5."*

(Marilyn Monroe)

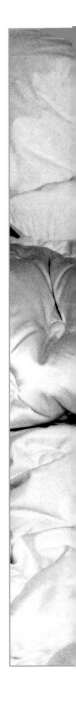

Sales soared, elevating what was already the most famous perfume in the world to legendary status. The American starlet and the French *eau de parfum* had a lasting connection that became even stronger after a shoot on March 24, 1955. Marilyn was more beautiful than ever when she posed with the famous bottle in her hotel room just before heading onstage at the Morosco Theatre on Broadway as the protagonist in Tennessee Williams's play *Cat on a Hot Tin Roof*. She would again pose next to the bottle in a series of photos taken for *Modern Screen* magazine, which scandalously shot her nude in bed. However, they were never published.

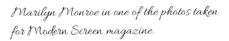

Marilyn Monroe in one of the photos taken for Modern Screen magazine.

As it achieved commercial success, Chanel No. 5 became a social
and cultural symbol. Coco had envisioned it as a modern sculpture, so it's no
surprise that its unusual, simple, and square form tickled the fantasy of artists.
The first to use it as a subject for his drawings was the French illustrator Sem,
who, after dedicating several cartoons in publications to Coco, recognized
the success of the perfume in 1921, drawing it in a way that was mistakenly
perceived to be an advertisement. In it, a young girl with hair and clothes
in perfect Chanel style looks up at a giant No. 5 bottle.

Chanel No. 5 appears for the first time in an illustration by Sem from 1921.

Je le déclare sans vergogne
Il n'y a rien de moins coco
Qu'une toilette de Coco
Parfumée à l'eau de Coco...
De coco... de cocologne

Marquise de la Flaconnerie

In 1923, Sem published a second illustration that depicted the stylist sitting in her atelier while surrounded by the unmistakable square outline of the perfume. Two decades later, Salvador Dali paid homage to his friend's creation with the piece *The Essence of Dali*, in which an ironic and irreverent mustache, similar to the one he had drawn on Leonardo da Vinci's *Mona Lisa*, stood out on a bottle that imitated the rectangular shape of Chanel No. 5. One of the most famous works of art inspired by the perfume was Andy Warhol's screen prints, which reinterpreted advertisements from 1954 to 1956 in the pop art style, a series entitled *Ads: Chanel*. At this point, the bottle had entered the collective imagination as a style icon and piece of design history. In 1959, it was added to the collections of the New York Museum of Modern Art.

Previous page: a satirical drawing by Sem from 1923 with a caricature of Coco inside an outline of the perfume bottle.

The Essence of Dali, a work of art by Salvador Dali that paid homage to Coco Chanel's perfume.

Ads: Chanel. Andy Warhol's screen print series from 1985 reinterprets 1950s advertisements for the perfume in the pop art style.

EVERYONE WANTS IT!
THE CHANEL SUPERSTARS

Catherine Deneuve for Chanel

A half a century of advertisements seen through the faces that represented the spirit of Mademoiselle's perfume. From Catherine Deneuve to Brad Pitt, the first male face of the famous women's perfume.

The image of Chanel No. 5 immediately brings to mind the impressive advertising campaigns that have fed its mythical status over time. But this wasn't always the case. If you were to flip through fashion magazines from the past, you would find that the story is much more compelling and complicated. In the first few decades, advertisement was rare and mediocre, and it was made even less effective due to competition with other Chanel perfumes that the company advertised at the same time as No. 5. They were all packaged and numbered in the exact same way. In short, many other perfumes followed No. 5: No. 22 in 1922 and, in the following years, Chanel No. 2, Chanel No. 7, Chanel No. 11, Chanel No. 14, Chanel No. 20, Chanel No. 21, and Chanel No. 27, as well as Gardénia, Bois des Îles, Cuir de Russie, Sycomore, Une Idée, and Jasmin. In 1955, there was Pour Monsieur cologne, and the latest perfume to be introduced under Coco's direction was No. 19 in 1970. But the only one to achieve great fame was No. 5. What was the secret to its fabulous destiny? The first advertisement that can be remembered wasn't used in France. It came out in the *New York Times*. It was a square frame in the corner of a page and showed the logo for the Bonwit Teller department stores where American women could find the latest Parisian fashions.

Previous pages: Catherine Deneuve photographed by Richard Avedon in 1972.

The original Chanel No. 5 bottle was on display at the MoMA in New York in 1959.

Coco Chanel, as the face of her perfume, poses in her suite at the Ritz Hotel in 1937.

Coco Chanel had seized the potential of the advertising world, but she knew that a new type of communication was necessary, one that was more direct and sharper, which would reflect the image of the strong, modern women who chose her perfume. Coco was the first to be the face of Chanel No. 5, photographed by François Kollar in her suite at the Ritz Hotel in Paris.

The image was published for the first time in *Harper's Bazaar* in 1937. In it, Mademoiselle posed while leaning on the fireplace and wearing a fabulous black dress in pure Chanel style. From then on, Maison Chanel always chose

Model Suzy Parker photographed by Richard Avedon in an advertisement from 1957.

beautiful starlets with innate class for the advertisements of its iconic perfume. They were made even more fascinating by the great photographers who were called to photograph the starlets and models. The challenge was in balancing the two spirits of a perfume that identifies itself as both the sophisticated icon of the elite and an object of mass desire. This declaration of intentions was summed up in the slogan chosen for the campaign with model Suzy Parker, a forerunner of the modern generation of supermodels, photographed by Richard Avedon in 1957. Next to the photo was the slogan "Every woman alive wants Chanel No. 5."

EAU DE TOILETTE N°5

CHANEL

Lauren Hutton poses in front of Richard Avedon's camera in 1967.

Right: Carole Bouquet photographed by Patrick Demarchelier in 1993.

Ten years later, Lauren Hutton, the famous actress from the film *A Wedding* by Robert Altman and *American Gigolo* with Richard Gere, posed for Richard Avedon for an unforgettable photo in which she jumps through the air in a short, pink pantsuit. Then it was the face of Catherine Deneuve that was chosen to represent the perfume in a series of photo campaigns directed by Helmut Newton, the sophisticated French star from *Belle de Jour* at its center.

Chanel No. 5 was also the first perfume to be advertised on television. On the small screen, Chanel's favorite face for the perfume was the actress Carole Bouquet, who appeared in a commercial by Ridley Scott and then in one by Bettina Rheims called *Sentiment Troublant* in the '90s. In it, she reads a monologue from the film *Gilda*. Patrick Demarchelier was then chosen to take photos of the actress for magazines.

PARFUM

N°5

CHANEL

PARIS

In the 1990s, director Jean-Paul Goude was called upon to change Chanel's image. He was a genius inventor of dreamlike fantasies, like the short film *Marilyn* from 1995, which reimagines the photo session with the Hollywood diva taken at the Ambassador Hotel forty years earlier. One of the brand's historic campaigns was the commercial entitled *Le Loup*, directed by Luc Besson and based on an illustrated storyboard by Milo Manara. Filmed in the Cinecittà Studios in Rome, it had Estella Warren as the lead playing Little Red Riding Hood trying to tame a wolf. Another distinctive commercial was filmed by Baz Luhrmann. It recalls his most famous film, *Moulin Rouge*, with Nicole Kidman as the star. On the set, she wore a black Karl Lagerfeld dress with her back exposed and a pendant with the No. 5 logo hanging behind her.

Ten years later, Chanel and Baz Luhrmann renewed their collaboration for another famous commercial. The protagonist chosen was Gisele Bündchen, an international star with natural beauty and modern femininity. She embodied the qualities of a new generation of women. Chanel decided to challenge tradition and launched a modern version of the perfume, one that was fresh and vibrant. Chanel asked perfumer Olivier Polge to redevelop the formula that it had created in 1921. He accepted the challenge and played with the classic notes of the bouquet to make it airier. It exalted the citrus hues of the aldehydes, the undertones were softened, and the ylang-ylang was greener.

N° 5

#THEONETHATIWANT

N°5
CHANEL
PARIS

PARFUM

One of the more memorable recent campaigns was *Train de Nuit* by Jean-Pierre Jeunet, the director of *Amélie*. It featured Audrey Tautou and evocative scenes set on the Orient Express. In 2012, the Maison shocked everyone when it had Brad Pitt star as the first male face of the women's perfume.

#CHANELN5

N°5
L'EAU

CHANEL

AVAILABLE ON CHANEL.COM

LEGEND OR TRUTH?

It's the most sold perfume of all time, one that everyone knows even if they've never used it. But many secrets hide behind it. Here are some things you probably didn't know about Chanel No. 5.

 AMERICAN SOLDIERS LINED UP IN PARIS TO BUY IT, BUT DURING WORLD WAR II, THE PERFUME WAS PRODUCED IN NEW JERSEY.

The Wertheimer brothers, who were Jewish, were majority partners in the Société des Parfums Chanel, which produced all the Maison's perfumes. In 1940, a few weeks before France's surrender, the Wertheimers left Paris to move to the United States. Continuing the production of Chanel No. 5 was a priority, so they set up a factory in Hoboken, New Jersey, and devised a reckless plan to get the rare floral essences needed to produce the perfume. From the United States, they sent their trusted man Gregory Thomas to France with the task of bringing back as much of the essence as possible. Gregory accomplished his mission and returned to the United States, smuggling rose and jasmine essences from the best plantations in Grasse. During the war, production of Chanel No. 5 never stopped, guaranteeing the quality of the original formula in every bottle.

THE SHAPE OF THE STOPPER
RECALLS A SQUARE IN PARIS.

Cut like a diamond, the stopper for the perfume is a copy of the perimeter of Place Vendôme. The octagonal square was built during Louis XIV's reign to frame a statue of the king. It was designed by Jules Hardouin-Mansart and is lined with historic palaces and the front of the Ritz Hotel, where Coco Chanel lived almost all her life.

THE ARCTIC COLD (ALSO) INSPIRED THE PERFUME.

When he presented the No. 5 blend to Coco Chanel, chemist Ernest Beaux told her he was inspired by the smell of winter, "by the marvelously fresh breeze that comes off lakes and rivers under the midnight sun." He said he had recreated the sensation he had during an expedition to the arctic, where he was sent as a soldier in World War I.

THERE IS A VERY RARE VERSION WITH A RED LABEL.

A cult object among collectors, the bottle was part of a small production that was used for Chanel No. 1, No. 2, and No. 31, in addition to No. 5. The bottles were set for production by Coco

Chanel in 1941 and were exclusively sold in the rue Cambon store until the end of the war.

CHANEL USED MADEMOISELLE CHANEL No. 31 AS HER PERSONAL PERFUME.

Coco stopped using No. 5 in the '40s after having used it for decades. She then chose No. 31 as her personal perfume, a musk blend with notes of jasmine and rose, which, after a few modifications, became the current No. 19. It was named for Coco's birthday, August 19, and began being sold just before her death in 1970.

EACH BOTTLE OF CHANEL No. 5 CONTAINS A THOUSAND JASMINE FLOWERS AND A DOZEN MAY ROSES.

In Pégomas, a few miles from Grasse, in the south of France, there are 50 acres (20 hectares) of fields where May roses bloom. They are exclusively used for Chanel, which puts them in its most famous perfume. The flowers are harvested by hand in the early morning as they bloom, which occurs for about 20 days, and they must be processed within an hour of harvesting.

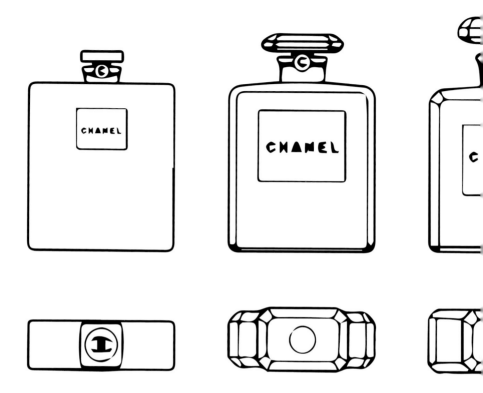

 ### THE BOTTLE HAS CHANGED SHAPE FIVE TIMES.

Initially, the perfume was not sold in the package you find it in today. The original bottle from 1921 had rounded edges and was slightly squarer. The first ones given to clients had a simple square glass stopper, whereas the octagonal cut one was created in 1924 when the thin and delicate glass of the first bottles were replaced by a thicker and stronger

version created by Cristalleries de Saint Louis, which also created a few valuable versions made of crystal. In the '50s, the stopper became wider, and in the '60s, it was made thicker. In 1986, it was reduced to balance out the proportions. The final change came in 1995 when the bottle returned to its original dimensions and the stopper was made slightly smaller.

Chiara Pasqualetti Johnson. A journalist from Milan, Chiara studied art history and now writes about travel, art, and lifestyle for major Italian publications. She has edited books and series about modern and contemporary art history. In 2018, she published *The Most Influential Women of Our Time*, an illustrated volume dedicated to the most influential female figures of the twentieth century, with White Star Publishers. It has been translated into twelve languages. In 2020, *Coco Chanel. Revolutionary Woman*, an illustrated biography about the queen of fashion, was published.

PHOTO CREDITS

p. 2: PLAINVIEW/Getty Images • p. 5: KAMMERMAN/Gamma-Rapho/Getty Images • p. 9: Studio Lipnitzki / Roger-Viollet/Alinari • pp. 10, 18, and 22: Musee Carnavalet/Roger Viollet/Getty Images (det.) • p. 13: Studio Lipnitzki/Roger Viollet/Alinari, Florence • pp. 14 and 17: Fine Art Images/Heritage Images/Getty Images • pp. 20–21: Cristopher Ames/Getty Images • p. 25: Eric Feferberg/AFP/Getty Images • pp. 26–27: Three Lions/Stringer/Hulton Archive/Getty Images • p. 29: Weeger (Arthur Felling) International Center of Photography/Getty Images • p. 30: Bridgeman Images • p. 31: Ed Feingersh/Michael Ochs Archives/Corbis/Getty Images • pp. 32–33: ARCHIVIO GBB/Alinari, Florence • p. 34: Pascal Le Segretain/Getty Images • p. 35: Musee Carnavalet/Roger Viollet/Getty Images • p. 36: Archives Charmet/Bridgeman Images • p. 37: Magnum Photos/Contrasto • p. 38: The Advertising Archives • p. 39: The Andy Warhol Foundation/Corbis/Getty Images • pp. 40–41: The Advertising Archives • p. 42: Eric Feferberg/AFP/Getty Images • p. 44: Private Collection • p. 45: The Advertising Archives • p. 46: Private Collection • p. 47: Grzegorz Czapski/Alamy Stock Photo • p. 48: The Advertising Archives • pp. 50–51: Retro Archives/Alamy Stock Photo • pp. 52, 53, 54-55: The Advertising Archive • pp. 56–57: Retro Archives/Alamy Stock Photo • p. 58: PLAINVIEW/Getty Images.

Editorial Project
Valeria Manferto De Fabianis

Graphic Design
Maria Cucchi

WS whitestar™ is a trademark property of White Star s.r.l.

© 2021 White Star s.r.l.
Piazzale Luigi Cadorna, 6
20123 Milan, Italy
www.whitestar.it

Translation: ICEIGeo, Milan (coordination: Lorenzo Sagripanti; translation: Alexa Ahern)
Editing: Abby Young

All rights reserved. No part of this publication may be reproduced, stored in a retrieval system, or transmitted in any form or by any means, including electronic, mechanical, photocopying, recording, or otherwise, without written permission from the publisher.

ISBN 978-88-544-1794-6
3 4 5 6 28 27 26 25 24

Printed in China